EMMANUEL JOSEPH

The Stage of Leadership, How Public Speaking and Action Drive Innovative Change

Copyright © 2025 by Emmanuel Joseph

All rights reserved. No part of this publication may be reproduced, stored or transmitted in any form or by any means, electronic, mechanical, photocopying, recording, scanning, or otherwise without written permission from the publisher. It is illegal to copy this book, post it to a website, or distribute it by any other means without permission.

First edition

*This book was professionally typeset on Reedsy.
Find out more at reedsy.com*

Contents

1	Chapter 1: The Essence of Leadership	1
2	Chapter 2: The Power of Public Speaking	3
3	Chapter 3: Action Speaks Louder Than Words	5
4	Chapter 4: Inspiring Innovative Change	7
5	Chapter 5: The Art of Storytelling	9
6	Chapter 6: The Role of Feedback in Leadership	11
7	Chapter 7: Building Trust and Credibility	13
8	Chapter 8: Navigating Change and Uncertainty	15
9	Chapter 9: Empowering Others	17
10	Chapter 10: The Value of Mentorship	19
11	Chapter 11: Leading with Emotional Intelligence	21
12	Chapter 12: The Importance of Vision and Strategy	23
13	Chapter 13: The Dynamics of Team Building	25
14	Chapter 14: Leading Through Conflict	27
15	Chapter 15: The Impact of Diversity and Inclusion	29
16	Chapter 16: The Balance of Work and Well-being	31
17	Chapter 17: The Legacy of Leadership	33

1

Chapter 1: The Essence of Leadership

Leadership transcends mere titles or roles; it's a dynamic stage where individuals impact and inspire others through their actions and words. At the heart of leadership lies the ability to envision a future that others may not yet see, making vision a crucial attribute. Vision gives leaders direction, providing a roadmap for their actions and decisions. However, vision alone is not enough; it must be accompanied by courage—the willingness to take risks, make tough decisions, and stand by one's principles even in the face of adversity. Courage propels leaders to act decisively, often setting them apart from others who may hesitate.

Moreover, true leadership is built on empathy, the ability to understand and share the feelings of others. Empathy connects leaders to their followers, fostering a sense of trust and loyalty. An empathetic leader can effectively communicate, resolve conflicts, and create an inclusive environment where everyone feels valued. Vision, courage, and empathy collectively form the core of effective leadership, enabling leaders to navigate complex challenges and inspire others to achieve common goals. Understanding these elements is the first step toward mastering the art of leadership and making a meaningful impact.

Leadership is not a static quality but a continuous journey of growth and development. Effective leaders are constantly learning, adapting, and evolving to meet the changing needs of their organizations and communities.

They seek feedback, reflect on their experiences, and are open to new ideas and perspectives. This commitment to personal and professional growth sets them apart and equips them to lead with confidence and competence. Leaders who embrace this mindset are better prepared to tackle the challenges of today and tomorrow, making them invaluable assets to their teams and organizations.

Ultimately, leadership is about making a difference. It's about inspiring others to reach their full potential, driving positive change, and leaving a lasting legacy. Whether it's through a powerful speech, a bold decision, or a compassionate gesture, leaders have the ability to transform lives and shape the future. Embracing the essence of leadership means recognizing the responsibility that comes with it and striving to make a positive impact in everything one does. As we explore the intricacies of leadership in this book, remember that the essence of leadership is within each of us, waiting to be harnessed and unleashed.

2

Chapter 2: The Power of Public Speaking

Public speaking stands as a cornerstone of effective leadership. Through powerful oratory, leaders communicate their vision, inspire action, and rally support. When a leader speaks with passion and conviction, the audience is moved not just by the content but by the authenticity behind the words. The ability to articulate a clear, compelling message can turn ideas into action, transforming abstract concepts into tangible outcomes. Public speaking, therefore, becomes a tool of influence, persuasion, and empowerment.

The impact of public speaking lies not only in the words but also in the delivery. A dynamic speaker uses body language, tone, and pacing to convey emotion and emphasis. Gestures, facial expressions, and eye contact create a connection with the audience, making the message more relatable and memorable. Practice and preparation are key, as they enable the speaker to deliver their message with confidence and clarity. A well-prepared speech, delivered with passion, can ignite a spark in the hearts of the listeners, driving them to take action and embrace change.

Moreover, public speaking serves as a platform for leaders to address challenges, share successes, and outline future plans. It is an opportunity to engage with stakeholders, build credibility, and foster a sense of unity and purpose. By addressing concerns, acknowledging contributions, and celebrating achievements, leaders can strengthen their relationship with their audience and create a shared sense of commitment. Effective public speaking bridges the gap between vision and action, turning aspirations into reality.

Ultimately, the power of public speaking lies in its ability to inspire and mobilize people. When leaders speak with passion, authenticity, and purpose, they create a ripple effect that extends beyond the immediate audience. Their words resonate, inspiring others to join the cause, take initiative, and drive change. In this way, public speaking becomes a catalyst for innovation, progress, and transformation, underscoring its significance in the realm of leadership.

3

Chapter 3: Action Speaks Louder Than Words

While words are powerful, actions often carry even greater weight. A leader's actions must align with their words, demonstrating integrity and authenticity. When leaders "walk the talk," they build credibility and trust with their followers. Consistency between words and actions reinforces the leader's commitment to their vision and values, inspiring others to do the same.

Taking action involves making decisions, implementing plans, and leading by example. It requires a proactive approach, where leaders anticipate challenges, seize opportunities, and drive progress. Leaders must be willing to take risks and embrace change, as innovation often demands stepping outside of one's comfort zone. By taking decisive action, leaders pave the way for others to follow, creating a culture of accountability and excellence.

Moreover, leaders who lead through action inspire their teams to achieve their full potential. They create an environment where initiative, creativity, and collaboration are encouraged and rewarded. By empowering team members to take ownership of their work and contribute to the collective goal, leaders foster a sense of purpose and motivation. This culture of action drives continuous improvement and innovation, propelling the organization forward.

In essence, actions speak louder than words because they demonstrate commitment and resolve. When leaders take action, they turn vision into reality, transforming ideas into tangible results. This alignment between words and actions builds trust, credibility, and loyalty, forming the foundation of effective leadership. By leading through action, leaders inspire others to follow suit, creating a ripple effect of positive change and progress.

4

Chapter 4: Inspiring Innovative Change

Innovation is the lifeblood of progress, and leaders play a crucial role in fostering a culture of innovation. This chapter explores how leaders can inspire innovative change by creating an environment that encourages creativity, collaboration, and continuous improvement. It starts with cultivating a growth mindset, where challenges are seen as opportunities for learning and development.

Leaders must empower their teams to experiment, take risks, and learn from failures. This involves providing the necessary resources, support, and autonomy for team members to explore new ideas and approaches. Additionally, leaders should recognize and celebrate innovative efforts, reinforcing the value of creativity within the organization. By championing innovation, leaders drive transformative change that propels their organizations forward.

Furthermore, leaders can inspire innovation by setting a clear vision and encouraging a sense of purpose among their teams. When team members understand the broader impact of their work, they are more likely to be motivated and engaged. Leaders should communicate the vision regularly, highlighting the importance of innovation in achieving the organization's goals. This alignment between vision and innovation fosters a sense of unity and direction, driving collective efforts toward meaningful change.

In conclusion, inspiring innovative change requires a combination of vision, empowerment, and celebration of creativity. Leaders who create an environment that nurtures these elements will see their organizations thrive in an ever-changing landscape. By embracing innovation and encouraging their teams to do the same, leaders pave the way for a future filled with possibilities and progress.

5

Chapter 5: The Art of Storytelling

Storytelling is a powerful tool in the leader's arsenal. It goes beyond mere communication, connecting with people on an emotional level and making messages more memorable and impactful. Through stories, leaders can illustrate their vision, share experiences, and convey complex ideas in a relatable and engaging manner. Storytelling humanizes leadership, making it accessible and inspiring.

An effective story has the power to captivate an audience, drawing them into the narrative and making them feel a part of the journey. It creates a sense of empathy, allowing the audience to see through the leader's eyes and understand their perspective. By sharing personal anecdotes, challenges, and triumphs, leaders can build trust and rapport with their audience, making their message more persuasive and influential.

Moreover, storytelling can be used to inspire action and drive change. By framing challenges as opportunities and successes as shared victories, leaders can motivate their teams to take initiative and strive for excellence. Stories of innovation, resilience, and collaboration can serve as powerful examples, encouraging others to embrace these values and contribute to the collective goal. In this way, storytelling becomes a catalyst for positive change and progress.

In essence, the art of storytelling lies in its ability to connect, inspire, and motivate. Leaders who master this art can effectively communicate their vision, build trust, and drive action. By weaving compelling narratives, they can turn abstract concepts into tangible realities, transforming ideas into impactful outcomes. As we explore the role of storytelling in leadership, remember that every leader has a story to tell, and it's through these stories that they can inspire and lead with purpose.

6

Chapter 6: The Role of Feedback in Leadership

Feedback is a vital tool in the leader's toolkit. It serves as a means of communication, providing insights into performance, behavior, and areas for improvement. Constructive feedback helps individuals understand their strengths and weaknesses, enabling them to grow and develop. For leaders, giving and receiving feedback is essential for fostering a culture of continuous improvement and excellence.

Effective feedback is specific, timely, and focused on behavior rather than personality. It should be delivered with empathy and respect, ensuring that the recipient feels valued and supported. Leaders who provide constructive feedback create an environment where team members are motivated to improve and excel. This feedback loop drives personal and professional growth, contributing to the overall success of the organization.

Receiving feedback is equally important for leaders. It provides valuable insights into their leadership style, decision-making, and impact on others. By seeking and embracing feedback, leaders demonstrate humility and a commitment to self-improvement. This openness to feedback fosters trust and collaboration, as team members feel heard and valued. Leaders who actively seek feedback are better equipped to adapt, innovate, and lead effectively in a rapidly changing world.

Ultimately, the role of feedback in leadership is to facilitate growth, learning, and improvement. It helps leaders and their teams to identify areas for development, set goals, and achieve their full potential. By creating a culture of feedback, leaders promote a continuous cycle of improvement, driving innovation and excellence. In this way, feedback becomes a powerful tool for driving change and achieving success.

7

Chapter 7: Building Trust and Credibility

Trust and credibility are the foundation of effective leadership. Without them, leaders cannot inspire, influence, or lead others. Trust is built through consistent actions, transparent communication, and integrity. Leaders who demonstrate honesty, reliability, and fairness earn the trust of their followers, creating a strong bond that fosters loyalty and commitment.

Credibility, on the other hand, is earned through expertise, competence, and consistency. Leaders who possess the knowledge and skills to make informed decisions and deliver results build credibility with their teams and stakeholders. Consistency in words and actions reinforces credibility, as it demonstrates the leader's commitment to their vision and values. Credible leaders are respected and trusted, making it easier for them to influence and lead others.

Building trust and credibility requires intentional effort and time. Leaders must be authentic, transparent, and accountable in their actions and decisions. They should communicate openly, share information, and involve others in the decision-making process. By doing so, they create a sense of ownership and buy-in, strengthening the trust and credibility they have built. This foundation of trust and credibility is essential for effective leadership and driving innovative change.

In essence, trust and credibility are the bedrock of leadership. They enable leaders to build strong relationships, inspire loyalty, and lead with confidence. By consistently demonstrating integrity, competence, and authenticity, leaders can earn the trust and credibility they need to drive change and achieve their goals. As we explore the importance of trust and credibility in leadership, remember that these qualities are earned through actions and behaviors, not just words.

8

Chapter 8: Navigating Change and Uncertainty

Change is a constant in today's world, and leaders must be adept at navigating it. Whether it's technological advancements, market shifts, or organizational restructuring, change presents both challenges and opportunities. Effective leaders embrace change, seeing it as a chance to innovate, grow, and improve. They understand that resistance to change can hinder progress, so they proactively address concerns, communicate the benefits, and involve others in the process.

Navigating change requires flexibility, adaptability, and resilience. Leaders must be open to new ideas and willing to pivot when necessary. They should encourage their teams to embrace change and see it as an opportunity for growth. This involves creating a culture where experimentation, risk-taking, and learning from failures are valued. By fostering a growth mindset, leaders can help their teams navigate change with confidence and optimism.

In times of uncertainty, leaders play a crucial role in providing stability and direction. Clear communication, transparency, and empathy are essential for guiding teams through uncertain times. Leaders should acknowledge the challenges and uncertainties, while also providing a vision and plan for the future. This helps to build trust and reassurance, enabling teams to stay focused and motivated despite the uncertainty.

Ultimately, navigating change and uncertainty is about being proactive, adaptable, and resilient. Leaders who embrace change and guide their teams through it can turn challenges into opportunities for innovation and growth. By fostering a culture of adaptability and continuous improvement, leaders can ensure their organizations thrive in an ever-changing landscape.

9

Chapter 9: Empowering Others

Empowerment is a key aspect of effective leadership. Empowered individuals are more engaged, motivated, and productive. Leaders who empower their team members create a culture of trust, ownership, and accountability. This involves providing the necessary resources, support, and autonomy for individuals to take initiative and make decisions. Empowered team members feel valued and trusted, which boosts their confidence and commitment to the organization's goals.

Empowerment begins with delegation. Leaders must delegate tasks and responsibilities, allowing team members to take ownership of their work. This not only frees up the leader's time but also provides opportunities for growth and development. Effective delegation involves clear communication, setting expectations, and providing the necessary support and resources. Leaders should also encourage team members to seek out new challenges and opportunities for learning.

Additionally, leaders should recognize and celebrate the contributions and achievements of their team members. This reinforces the value of their work and encourages continued effort and excellence. Recognition can take many forms, from public acknowledgment to rewards and incentives. By celebrating success, leaders create a positive and motivating environment where individuals feel appreciated and motivated to perform at their best.

Empowerment is about creating a culture where individuals are encouraged to take initiative, make decisions, and contribute to the organization's success. Leaders who empower their teams build trust, foster innovation, and drive continuous improvement. In this way, empowerment becomes a powerful tool for achieving organizational goals and driving positive change.

10

Chapter 10: The Value of Mentorship

Mentorship is a crucial aspect of leadership, providing guidance, support, and development opportunities for both the mentor and the mentee. Through mentorship, leaders can share their knowledge, experience, and insights with others, helping them navigate their career paths and achieve their goals. A strong mentorship relationship fosters trust, mutual respect, and personal growth.

Mentors play a vital role in identifying and nurturing talent within an organization. They provide valuable feedback, offer career advice, and help mentees develop the skills and confidence needed to succeed. By investing in the growth and development of others, mentors contribute to the overall success and resilience of the organization. Additionally, mentorship allows leaders to pass on their legacy, ensuring that their values, knowledge, and vision continue to shape the organization long after they are gone.

For mentees, having a mentor provides a unique opportunity to learn from someone who has been there before. They gain valuable insights into the challenges and opportunities that lie ahead, as well as guidance on how to navigate them. Mentorship helps mentees develop their leadership skills, build their professional network, and achieve their career aspirations. It is a mutually beneficial relationship that promotes growth, development, and success.

Ultimately, the value of mentorship lies in its ability to foster learning, growth, and development. Leaders who prioritize mentorship create a culture of continuous improvement and excellence within their organizations. They build strong, supportive relationships that inspire and empower others to reach their full potential. In this way, mentorship becomes a powerful tool for driving positive change and achieving organizational success.

11

Chapter 11: Leading with Emotional Intelligence

Emotional intelligence (EI) is a critical component of effective leadership. It involves the ability to recognize, understand, and manage one's own emotions, as well as the emotions of others. Leaders with high emotional intelligence are better equipped to build strong relationships, resolve conflicts, and create a positive work environment. They are empathetic, self-aware, and capable of regulating their emotions in a way that fosters trust and collaboration.

One key aspect of emotional intelligence is self-awareness. Leaders must be aware of their own emotions, strengths, and weaknesses. This self-awareness allows them to respond to situations with composure and confidence, rather than reacting impulsively. Self-aware leaders are also more open to feedback and willing to make adjustments to improve their leadership effectiveness.

Another important component of emotional intelligence is empathy. Empathetic leaders can understand and share the feelings of others, creating a sense of connection and trust. They listen actively, show compassion, and respond to the needs and concerns of their team members. Empathy helps leaders build strong, supportive relationships and fosters a positive work culture where individuals feel valued and understood.

In essence, leading with emotional intelligence involves being attuned to one's own emotions and the emotions of others. It requires self-awareness, empathy, and the ability to regulate emotions effectively. Leaders who prioritize emotional intelligence create a positive, collaborative work environment where individuals feel supported and motivated to perform at their best. By leading with emotional intelligence, leaders can drive positive change and achieve organizational success.

12

Chapter 12: The Importance of Vision and Strategy

Vision and strategy are fundamental elements of effective leadership. Vision provides direction and inspiration, while strategy outlines the steps needed to achieve that vision. Together, they form the foundation for decision-making, goal-setting, and action. Leaders who can articulate a clear vision and develop a coherent strategy are better equipped to guide their organizations toward success.

A compelling vision paints a picture of the desired future state, inspiring and motivating others to work toward it. It serves as a guiding light, providing clarity and focus in times of uncertainty. Leaders must communicate their vision effectively, ensuring that everyone understands and buys into it. This shared vision creates a sense of purpose and unity, driving collective efforts toward achieving the organization's goals.

Strategy, on the other hand, is the roadmap for achieving the vision. It involves setting specific, measurable objectives and outlining the actions needed to reach them. A well-developed strategy takes into account the organization's strengths, weaknesses, opportunities, and threats. It provides a clear plan of action, ensuring that resources are allocated effectively and progress is monitored and evaluated.

In essence, vision and strategy are critical components of leadership. They provide direction, focus, and a sense of purpose, guiding the organization toward its goals. Leaders who can articulate a compelling vision and develop a coherent strategy are better equipped to navigate challenges, seize opportunities, and drive positive change. By prioritizing vision and strategy, leaders can achieve organizational success and leave a lasting impact.

13

Chapter 13: The Dynamics of Team Building

Team building is an essential aspect of leadership, fostering collaboration, trust, and a sense of belonging. Effective team building involves creating an environment where individuals feel valued, supported, and motivated to contribute to the collective goal. Leaders who prioritize team building create a strong, cohesive team that is capable of achieving exceptional results.

One key aspect of team building is establishing clear roles and responsibilities. Leaders must ensure that each team member understands their role and how it contributes to the overall success of the team. This clarity helps to prevent misunderstandings, reduce conflicts, and improve efficiency. Additionally, leaders should encourage open communication and collaboration, ensuring that everyone feels comfortable sharing ideas and feedback.

Trust is another critical component of team building. Leaders must build trust by demonstrating integrity, reliability, and fairness in their actions and decisions. Trust fosters a sense of psychological safety, where individuals feel comfortable taking risks and expressing their opinions. By building trust, leaders create a supportive environment where team members feel valued and motivated to perform at their best.

In conclusion, the dynamics of team building involve creating a supportive, collaborative environment where individuals feel valued and motivated to contribute to the collective goal. Leaders who prioritize team building foster trust, open communication, and a sense of belonging within their teams. By building strong, cohesive teams, leaders can drive exceptional results and achieve organizational success.

14

Chapter 14: Leading Through Conflict

Conflict is an inevitable part of any organization, and effective leaders must be adept at managing and resolving it. Conflict can arise from differences in opinions, goals, or values, and if left unaddressed, it can hinder progress and damage relationships. Leaders who navigate conflict with skill and empathy can transform it into an opportunity for growth and improvement.

The first step in leading through conflict is to understand its root causes. Leaders must listen actively to all parties involved, seeking to understand their perspectives and concerns. This empathetic approach helps to build trust and create a safe space for open dialogue. By acknowledging and validating the feelings of others, leaders can diffuse tension and pave the way for constructive conversation.

Once the root causes are understood, leaders can facilitate a resolution by encouraging collaboration and compromise. They should guide the parties involved toward finding common ground and mutually beneficial solutions. This may involve negotiating, mediating, or seeking input from a neutral third party. The goal is to reach an agreement that addresses the concerns of all parties and promotes a positive outcome.

Ultimately, leading through conflict requires a combination of empathy, communication, and problem-solving skills. Leaders who can navigate conflict effectively create a harmonious and collaborative work environment.

They demonstrate that differences can be resolved constructively, fostering a culture of respect and cooperation. By embracing conflict as an opportunity for growth, leaders can strengthen their teams and drive organizational success.

15

Chapter 15: The Impact of Diversity and Inclusion

Diversity and inclusion are essential components of effective leadership and organizational success. A diverse workforce brings a wide range of perspectives, experiences, and ideas, which can drive innovation and creativity. Inclusive leaders create an environment where everyone feels valued, respected, and empowered to contribute their unique strengths.

Embracing diversity starts with recognizing and appreciating the differences among individuals. Leaders must actively seek to understand and value the diverse backgrounds, cultures, and perspectives of their team members. This involves creating opportunities for open dialogue and fostering a culture of respect and inclusion. By valuing diversity, leaders can tap into the full potential of their teams and drive better decision-making and problem-solving.

Inclusion, on the other hand, involves creating a sense of belonging for all team members. Inclusive leaders ensure that everyone has an equal opportunity to participate, contribute, and succeed. They actively address barriers to inclusion, such as biases and stereotypes, and promote fairness and equity in all aspects of the organization. By fostering an inclusive environment, leaders create a sense of belonging and motivation, driving engagement and performance.

In essence, diversity and inclusion are not just moral imperatives but strategic advantages. Leaders who prioritize diversity and inclusion build stronger, more innovative, and resilient organizations. They create a culture where everyone feels valued and empowered to contribute their best. By embracing diversity and fostering inclusion, leaders can drive positive change and achieve organizational success.

16

Chapter 16: The Balance of Work and Well-being

Effective leadership involves recognizing the importance of work-life balance and well-being. Leaders who prioritize the well-being of their team members create a positive and supportive work environment. This involves promoting work-life balance, encouraging self-care, and addressing factors that contribute to stress and burnout.

Promoting work-life balance starts with setting clear boundaries and expectations. Leaders should encourage their team members to take breaks, manage their workload, and prioritize their well-being. This may involve implementing flexible work arrangements, providing resources for stress management, and promoting a healthy work-life integration. By prioritizing work-life balance, leaders create a more motivated, engaged, and productive workforce.

In addition to promoting work-life balance, leaders must also address factors that contribute to stress and burnout. This involves recognizing the signs of burnout and taking proactive steps to address them. Leaders should provide support and resources for mental health and well-being, such as counseling services, wellness programs, and stress management workshops. By addressing these factors, leaders create a supportive and healthy work environment.

Ultimately, the balance of work and well-being is essential for long-term success. Leaders who prioritize the well-being of their team members create a positive and supportive work environment. They recognize that a healthy, happy workforce is more engaged, productive, and resilient. By promoting work-life balance and well-being, leaders can drive organizational success and create a culture of care and support.

17

Chapter 17: The Legacy of Leadership

The final chapter explores the lasting impact of leadership—the legacy that leaders leave behind. A leader's legacy is shaped by their actions, decisions, and the positive change they inspire. It is a reflection of their vision, values, and the difference they make in the lives of others. Leaders who leave a lasting legacy create a positive and enduring impact on their organizations, communities, and the world.

A leader's legacy begins with their vision and values. Leaders who articulate a clear and compelling vision inspire others to work toward a common goal. This vision becomes a guiding light, shaping the actions and decisions of the leader and their team. Leaders who uphold their values, demonstrate integrity, and lead by example create a positive and lasting impact on their organization and its culture.

The legacy of leadership is also shaped by the relationships leaders build and the people they inspire. Leaders who invest in the growth and development of others create a ripple effect of positive change. They empower their team members to achieve their full potential, fostering a culture of continuous improvement and excellence. The impact of these relationships and the positive change they inspire extend far beyond the leader's tenure.

In essence, the legacy of leadership is a reflection of the positive change and lasting impact leaders create. It is shaped by their vision, values, actions, and the people they inspire. Leaders who prioritize making a positive difference create a lasting legacy that endures long after they are gone. As we conclude this book, remember that leadership is not just about the present but about creating a positive and lasting impact on the future.

The Stage of Leadership: How Public Speaking and Action Drive Innovative Change is a compelling exploration of the intricate relationship between leadership, communication, and action. This book delves into the essential qualities that define great leaders, highlighting the importance of vision, courage, and empathy. Through a comprehensive analysis, the book emphasizes the pivotal role of public speaking in conveying a leader's vision, inspiring action, and rallying support.

The author explores the profound impact that effective communication can have in turning ideas into reality, transforming abstract concepts into tangible outcomes. Furthermore, the book underscores the significance of aligning words with actions, demonstrating how leaders who "walk the talk" build trust, credibility, and foster a culture of accountability and excellence. By leading through action, leaders pave the way for innovation and progress, inspiring their teams to follow suit.

A key theme in the book is the role of storytelling in leadership. Through captivating narratives, leaders can connect with their audience, making messages more memorable and impactful. The book also explores the importance of mentorship, emotional intelligence, diversity, inclusion, and work-life balance in shaping effective leadership. It provides practical strategies for navigating change and conflict, building trust and credibility, and empowering others to achieve their full potential.

In essence, **The Stage of Leadership** is a comprehensive guide that equips leaders with the tools and insights needed to drive innovative change. It is an inspiring read for anyone looking to enhance their leadership skills and make a meaningful impact. Through its exploration of the multifaceted nature of leadership, the book offers valuable lessons and actionable strategies for leaders at all levels.

www.ingramcontent.com/pod-product-compliance
Lightning Source LLC
LaVergne TN
LVHW020459080526
838202LV00057B/6055